Remembering Manzanar

Life in a Japanese Relocation Camp

Michael L. Cooper

Clarion Books / New York

Clarion Books
a Houghton Mifflin Company imprint
215 Park Avenue South, New York, NY 10003
Copyright © 2002 by Michael L. Cooper

The text was set in 13-point Centaur MT.

For information about permission to reproduce selections from this book, write to Permissions,
Houghton Mifflin Company, 215 Park Avenue South, New York, NY 10003.

www.houghtonmifflinbooks.com

Printed in the USA.

Library of Congress Cataloging-in-Publication Data

Cooper, Michael L., 1950–
Remembering Manzanar : life in a Japanese relocation camp / by Michael Cooper.
p. cm.
Summary: Uses firsthand accounts, oral histories, and essays from school newspapers and yearbooks to tell the
story of the Japanese Americans who were sent to live in government-run internment camps during World War II.
Includes bibliographical references and index.
ISBN 0-618-06778-7
1. Manzanar War Relocation Center—History—Sources—Juvenile literature.
2. Japanese Americans—Evacuation and relocation, 1942–1945—Juvenile literature.
3. Concentration camps—United States—History—Sources—Juvenile literature.
[1. Manzanar War Relocation Center—History—Sources.
2. Japanese Americans—Evacuation and relocation, 1942–1945. 3. World War, 1939-1945—United States.]
I. Title.
D769.8.A6 C67 2002
940.54'72773'0979487—dc21
2002002745

RO 10 9 8 7 6 5 4 3 2 1

To Allen Jensen

Special thanks to Aloha South of the National Archives, Cameron Trowbridge and Marie Masumoto of the Japanese American National Museum, and former Manzanar evacuees Sue Kunitomi Embrey and Wilbur Sato.

CONTENTS

A grandfather and his grandson. DOROTHEA LANGE/NATIONAL ARCHIVES

Introduction

When Japan pushed America into World War II with its devastating surprise air attack on the U.S. Navy and Army Air Force bases at Pearl Harbor, Hawaii, the FBI suspected Japanese American communities of harboring spies and saboteurs. Two months after the December 7, 1941, attack, the president of the United States signed Executive Order 9066, which gave Army generals the authority to begin a forced, mass evacuation of all people of Japanese ancestry from the three West Coast states—Washington, Oregon, and California. In all, the Army uprooted 112,353 people from their schools, jobs, and homes. It was the largest forced evacuation in American history.

Almost 41,000 of those West Coast residents were middle-aged and elderly Japanese aliens who, as young men and women, had immigrated to America early in the twentieth century. These immigrants were called Issei, a Japanese word that means "first generation." None of the Issei were American citizens, because U.S. law did not allow Asian immigrants to become citizens. The rest of the 71,000 plus people were the children and grandchildren of the Issei. The children were called Nisei, the Japanese word for "second generation," and the grandchildren were called Sansei, which means "third generation." Born in the United States, the Nisei and Sansei were American citizens.

The Army sent Japanese immigrants and Japanese Americans alike to crowded assembly centers, usually fairgrounds, near their former homes. Then, in early April 1942, the Army began moving everyone by train and bus to ten isolated war relocation centers, each one the size of a small city.

The first Japanese Americans ordered from their homes were moved to an Owens Valley relocation center named Manzanar, in eastern California's high desert. Today Manzanar is a National Historic Site operated by the National Park Service and visited by tens of thousands of people each year.

The Photographers

Noted photographers Dorothea Lange and Ansel Adams took many of the photographs shown in this book.

Dorothea Lange lived in California and worked for the federal government as a photographer. It was her job to photograph the evacuation and the relocation camps. She first visited Manzanar in April 1942, while people were still moving into the camp. Lange's photographs, unlike those later taken by Adams, show the anxiety in the faces of men and women recently forced from their homes. Her photographs have appeared in so many books, newspapers, magazines, and documentaries that they have shaped the popular image of the evacuation.

Ansel Adams is best known for his nature photography, especially of Yosemite National Park, near his home in the Sierra Nevada. In the fall of 1943 Manzanar's director, Ralph P. Merritt, invited Adams to photograph the camp. Adams focused his camera on the gardens, the parks, the schools, and the other improvements that had been made by the hard-working Issei and Nisei. The people he photographed look happy and industrious, as though they had few cares in the world. Adams published his photographs in 1944 in a book titled *Born Free and Equal.* War was still raging in the Pacific,

Toyo Miyatake. ANSEL ADAMS/LIBRARY OF CONGRESS

and most Americans hated the Japanese. And they hated Adams's book. Some even burned it.

The government employed other photographers to document the evacuation and the relocation camps. Clem Albers, Russell Lee, and Francis Stewart took numerous photographs of Manzanar, and their work appears in this book.

One of the few people to take unofficial photographs at Manzanar was confined there. Toyo Miyatake was a professional photographer from Los Angeles. When Miyatake and his family were moved to Manzanar in April 1942, he smuggled in film and a camera lens. He later made a camera box so that he could take pictures of the camp. Ralph Merritt discovered Miyatake's camera but let him continue taking photographs, with one stipulation: Miyatake could not actually *take* the picture. He could set up his camera and compose the shot, but a staff person had to press the shutter button.

Every photographer of Manzanar had to choose his or her subjects carefully, because Army censors inspected all photographs. They did not allow pictures of angry residents, soldiers with guns, barbed-wire fences, or guard towers. But a few people managed to sneak photographs of these subjects past the censors.

Most of the photographs in this book come from the Library of Congress or the National Archives, where there are more than 12,500 photographs of the evacuation, the assembly centers, and the ten relocation camps.

The entrance to Manzanar National Historic Site. MICHAEL L. COOPER

I

The Annual Manzanar Pilgrimage

The Manzanar Pilgrimage began in 1969. Each year since then, hundreds of people have made a special trip to the old relocation camp in the Owens Valley. Some young men and women observe the event by participating in a relay run, covering the 225 miles from Los Angeles in five days. But most visitors travel by bus or by car.

I drove a rental car to the annual Manzanar Pilgrimage on Saturday, April 28, 2001. I enjoyed the scenic drive north from Los Angeles International Airport to the mountains of eastern California, and I was filled with anticipation by the time I reached the small town of Lone Pine at the southern end of the valley. This was where thousands of Japanese Americans had arrived by train and set foot for the first time on Owens Valley sand. Buses had then driven them the final nine miles to the Manzanar Relocation Camp.

As I sped along the same stretch of highway, I tried to imagine the anxiety and apprehension the people on those buses must have felt. The landscape has changed little, if at all. The snow-capped Sierra Nevada dominate the western horizon. Scrub and brush grow in the flat expanses on either side of the highway. After the eighth mile, I sat up higher in the car seat, eager for my first glimpse of the internment camp.

This photograph of a dust storm at Manzanar is one of Lange's most famous photographs.
DOROTHEA LANGE/NATIONAL ARCHIVES

From the highway little can be seen. A pair of stone pagoda-style sentry houses divides the hard-packed dirt road leading into the camp. There is only one other building, several hundred yards away. It is the green auditorium that camp residents had constructed in 1943. Thousands of people drive by this spot without knowing what happened here during World War II. "Probably some old Army base," they might mutter as they speed by the sentry posts.

For people unfamiliar with the past, there is little here to see. But for those who know the history of this place called Manzanar, there is much to observe.

2

I parked my car on the side of the road. Opening the door, I felt the strong, cool wind that always seems to be blowing through the valley. Grains of sand carried by the wind stung my face. In the distance, against the Sierra Nevada, I noticed an elderly man standing alone amid the sage. He was gazing westward. I imagined he was a former Manzanar resident recalling the pain and confusion of his boyhood years here. Or perhaps he was remembering the many times he had stood on that same spot, staring at the tall mountains and wishing he could fly over them, back to his home near the ocean.

I knew that the Manzanar Pilgrimage could be very emotional for the former evacuees, their families, and friends. While researching the history of Manzanar, I read a newspaper story about the 1997 pilgrimage. The article described a young man named Matthew Narita, who said his grandfather had died just a few months earlier. Matthew's grandfather had been confined at Manzanar, and his death had made the grandson's visit especially sad. "We planted flags," Matthew said, "and I was crying and it was just crazy."

He explained that the forced evacuation in 1942 had harmed not only his grandparents but their children and their children's children as well. "The Japanese heritage of my family," he said, "was wiped out, because they were so ashamed." Shame silenced many people who were confined in the relocation camps. Their children and grandchildren attend the annual pilgrimage to learn more about their past.

It is easy to understand why Japanese Americans want to know what happened in this war relocation camp. But why is it important for other Americans to remember Manzanar?

Japanese Americans leaving their homes in San Pedro, near Los Angeles Harbor. CLEM ALBERS/NATIONAL ARCHIVES

2

Evacuation

Just hours after the early-morning bombing of Pearl Harbor, FBI agents rushed to Fish Harbor, a community of commercial fishermen on Terminal Island in Los Angeles Harbor. Some three thousand Japanese immigrants and their American-born children lived there. The agents suspected them of spying for the enemy or plotting to bomb Long Beach Naval Shipyard, which shared part of the island.

The fishermen had been living on the island since the 1920s. The men worked on their own fishing boats or as crew on other people's boats. Their wives held jobs in local fish canneries. Nisei children attended Terminal Island elementary schools or rode the ferry to high school on the mainland. It was a hard-working community, in which the Japanese coexisted with immigrants from the Philippines, Poland, and Mexico. But that changed abruptly after Pearl Harbor. The Fish Harbor residents were among the first people to feel the harsh measures imposed against Japanese Americans at the beginning of World War II.

"The entire atmosphere of Terminal Island was . . . just plain panicky," recalled a Nisei woman who had grown up on the island and, at age eighteen, was sent to Manzanar. "On the street, persons with whom we used to speak

Boats that belonged to Japanese fishermen in the harbor at Terminal Island. There are FOR SALE *signs on several of the boats.* NATIONAL ARCHIVES

and joke looked to me as strangers," the woman explained. "It was very difficult to smile—nobody did! There were people talking in groups; there were people hurrying to and from, all greatly disturbed. Soon the whole island was filled with soldiers, machine guns, and jeeps. They started breaking up the chattering groups of people."

A Nisei fisherman described how nearly two months after Pearl Harbor federal agents returned to Terminal Island and arrested his father and hundreds of other men. "On February 1 or 2, about six hundred men were taken in. The FBI came and took them. Of all the older men, only a few, mostly businessmen, were left, perhaps twenty or so. They were taken to the immigration station. They thought they would be questioned and released. . . .

Then, one or two days later, families were notified to send clothes to the immigration center. Then we knew it would be longer."

Life was difficult for the people remaining in Fish Harbor. Other fishermen cursed them. The canneries fired the women from their jobs. The military disconnected their telephones, closed their businesses, and did not let them withdraw money from their bank accounts. Soldiers and sailors guarded the island's one bridge and the ferryboats to the mainland. The guards made Nisei teenagers show identification when they boarded the ferries back and forth to high school. Once, soldiers detained a group of students all day. The incident scared the young people, and many quit going to school.

"Our mother was afraid to let us go anywhere," said the Nisei woman. "We heard rumors that some Japanese people were being attacked and killed; we read horrible news of arson." The Fish Harbor residents began running out of money with which to buy food and pay the rent on their homes. Just

A soldier patrols a street in Fish Harbor where Japanese immigrants once lived. NATIONAL ARCHIVES

as these people thought their lives could not get any worse, they did. More bad news arrived on February 26.

"We were having our supper when a Marine came around delivering notices," the woman said. "As my sister finished reading aloud the one handed to us, nobody uttered a word; we stood motionless, staring blankly—we

Evacuees boarding a train before dawn in downtown Los Angeles. RUSSELL LEE/LIBRARY OF CONGRESS

were all dumbfounded. That was the notice that ordered us out of our home in forty-eight hours."

Few families owned cars or could afford movers, so they were forced to sell or abandon their belongings. "Junk men swarmed over the island," the fisherman said. "They were there to make bargains with the evacuees, bargains that would have been laughed at on ordinary days. . . . Any price, even though outrageously low, was better than leaving the household furniture and other belongings lying in the house to be stolen.

"We sold most of our own property to junk men—table, chairs, bureau, a couple of beds, a stove, and radio. We got fifty dollars for what we sold. If we had bought it at a secondhand store, it would have cost three hundred dollars. If we had bought it new, it would have cost seven to eight hundred dollars."

The eighteen-year-old woman described her feelings those last two days before evacuation. "The precious forty-eight hours passed like a nightmare. The last night, I took a final glance through the rooms in which we had slept and eaten ever since I could remember. . . . I wanted to cry, but my eyes were dry. Even now my memories go back to my dear home, but never again will we be able to go back to it, I know." She was right. There was never another Japanese American community on Terminal Island.

Finding new homes proved difficult. "Practically all places were taken, or it was the story of 'No room for Japs' or 'Families with children not allowed,'" the woman recalled. "Hotels in Little Tokyo were all packed to capacity."

The fisherman explained that "people who had relatives and friends went to them. Then, people who didn't have any place to go were offered shelter at churches," which included Christian churches as well as traditional Japanese churches—Buddhist, Shinto, and Tenrikyo.

"Our family lived with others in a language school building," the fisher-

A family waiting to board their train. Their bags and suitcases were packed with clothing and a few personal items. RUSSELL LEE/LIBRARY OF CONGRESS

man said, describing their crowded, makeshift home. "All the males were in one room, all the women in another. . . . This is the way we lived for about a month. So many women would cook one day and so many another. The work was all divided."

As the former Fish Harbor residents were still adjusting to their new homes, the government announced that they had to move again.

President Franklin D. Roosevelt had signed Executive Order 9066 in February 1942. It authorized the Army to force everyone of Japanese heritage to leave the West Coast. Then, on March 18, the president signed Executive Order 9102, authorizing the creation of the War Relocation Authority (WRA), a federal agency that would operate ten large camps, where all the Japanese and Japanese Americans from the three West Coast states would be taken and confined.

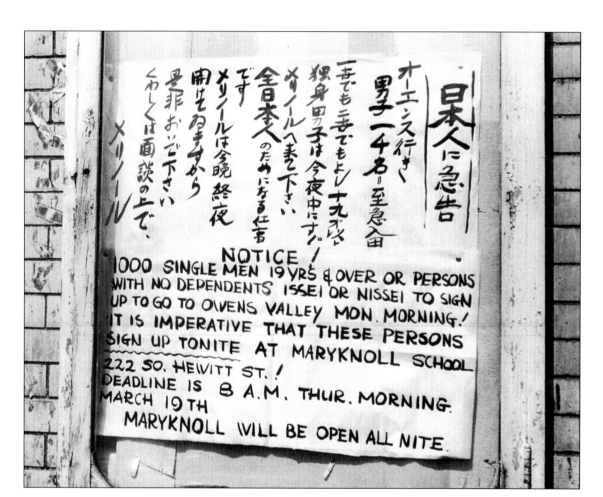

Surprisingly, nearly one thousand men did volunteer to help build the relocation camp. They wanted to prove their loyalty to the United States. RUSSELL LEE/LIBRARY OF CONGRESS

3

The First Months at Manzanar

The same week that Roosevelt created the WRA, workers in the Owens Valley began clearing land for the first camp. They called it Manzanar, a Spanish word that means "apple orchard." Manzanar was the name of a small community of fruit growers who had lived there two decades earlier.

The camp "will furnish the Japanese with every comfort except the bright lights of Little Tokyo," the *Los Angeles Times* stated confidently. The majority of people of Japanese ancestry in America lived in southern California. And Little Tokyo, in downtown Los Angeles, was where many of them went to shop and socialize. It was a lively and prosperous community, with movie theaters, hotels, restaurants, and department stores. Few Japanese Americans believed Manzanar would be as inviting as Little Tokyo.

After hearing rumors that the Owens Valley was crawling with rattlesnakes and stinging fire ants, families spent precious time before evacuation rushing from store to store, searching for boots. Others were told that Manzanar mosquitoes were as big as birds, and they bought yards of mosquito netting. And someone said men and women had to share showers, so the girls packed bathing suits.

One persistent rumor was frightening. If the Japanese Army attacked the mainland, some people said, American planes would bomb Manzanar and kill the inhabitants in retaliation. Could that be possible? It was hard to believe. But before Pearl Harbor, few Japanese Americans would have thought that their government would imprison them because of their heritage. They did not know what or whom to believe anymore.

Eager to prove their loyalty to the United States, hundreds of people volunteered to relocate early and help build the Manzanar camp. The first eighty-one volunteers, sixty-one men and twenty women, arrived on March 21, 1942. A week later, at sunrise, more than seven hundred additional volunteers left Pasadena in a four-mile-long convoy. A jeep carrying Major C. V. Cadwell, the Army officer in charge, led the way. It was followed by a Model T driven by Haro Yameamote, a fifty-four-year-old gardener. Behind

Convoy of volunteers arriving on March 28, 1942. LIBRARY OF CONGRESS

Construction begins on Manzanar in the remote Owens Valley. LIBRARY OF CONGRESS

him were 238 cars and trucks packed with suitcases, boxes, garden tools, ironing boards, and tomato plants. The convoy could travel along Highway 395 only as fast as the slowest car, thirty miles an hour, so it did not reach the Owens Valley until late afternoon.

The newcomers first noticed the land's emptiness and stark beauty. The Sierra Nevada, their jagged ten-thousand-foot peaks piercing the sky, create a high wall on the western side of the long valley. The Inyo Mountains form a less imposing wall on the eastern side. Sage, manzanita, rabbit brush, and black locust, Joshua, and cottonwood trees grow on the wide valley floor between the two mountain ranges.

At the construction site the volunteers slept in canvas tents and worked beside hundreds of Caucasian carpenters and laborers ten hours a day, six days a week, hammering together rows of simple, single-story buildings. The workers completed an average of twenty buildings a day. But that was not fast enough, and the first people who moved into the camp had to live in crowded, poorly constructed barracks.

Two weeks after construction began, thousands of men, women, and children began arriving by train and bus. There were one thousand new arrivals on April 3 and nine hundred more the next day. Three thousand people arrived on April 25. On the last two days of April and the first day of May, nearly three thousand people moved into the camp. Some of these newcomers came from San Francisco and Palo Alto. The Army brought more than two

Partially finished camp in April 1942. LIBRARY OF CONGRESS

Boys at the train station. The tags dangling from their coats are marked with their family's identification number, which had been assigned by the Army. RUSSELL LEE/LIBRARY OF CONGRESS

hundred strawberry farmers from Bainbridge Island in Washington State. But most of the 10,046 people sent to Manzanar were from southern California towns and communities such as Burbank, Glendale, Hollywood, Long Beach, San Pedro, Santa Monica, Venice, and West Los Angeles.

Buses carrying evacuees from the Lone Pine train station stopped in front of the camp's administration building. New arrivals stood in line for up to two hours, waiting for the authorities to record their names, give each new WRA identification numbers, and assign each family a room. Doctors and nurses then gave everyone a typhoid shot and a quick physical examination. Next, each newcomer picked up two rough woolen Army blankets. Afterward, people

A young family getting off the bus at Manzanar in April 1942. CLEM ALBERS/NATIONAL ARCHIVES

People registered with camp officials as soon as they arrived. LIBRARY OF CONGRESS

located their luggage amid the jumble of suitcases and boxes on the ground. Soldiers searched each bag for contraband—forbidden items such as cameras or books written in Japanese. Finally, the evacuees went to find their rooms.

Few people ever forgot their first impression of the barracks. Sue Kunitomi Embrey described the night she and her family came to Manzanar. Sue was a teenager in 1942, living with her two sisters, five brothers, and mother in downtown Los Angeles, near Little Tokyo. Sue's father had died in an automobile accident four years earlier. One of Sue's brothers had gone to the Owens Valley camp in March as a volunteer laborer. The rest of the family was ordered to leave their home on the first Sunday in May 1942. After a ten-hour train ride, they arrived at Manzanar at the end of the day.

"It was already dark," Sue said, "and after registering in one of the large barracks, my brother, who had volunteered in March to work at Manzanar, escorted us with one flashlight through the darkness to our barracks in block 20, which was sort of in the middle of the camp. It was cold and dark and very quiet except for the shuffling of our feet on the uneven ground; very difficult to see anything without light.

"My brother had already filled the ticking with hay for our beds, which were canvas Army cots. There were eight of them, and one light bulb hanging from the ceiling. My mother sat down on one of the cots and said in Japanese, 'To a place like this?' We were pretty shocked at the bare room—no insulation, no linoleum, planks with knotholes, and the wind blowing through the top where the roof peaked. We heard voices from next door.

Nurses giving typhoid vaccinations. CLEM ALBERS/NATIONAL ARCHIVES

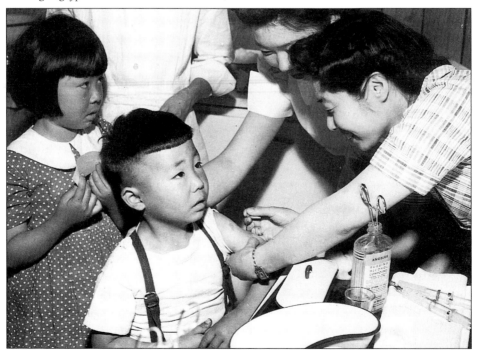

My mom, pop, & me

Us living three

Dreaded the day

When we rode away,

Away to the land

With lots of sand

My mom, pop, & me.

The day of evacuation,

We left our little station

Leaving our friends

And my tree that bends

Away to the land

With lots of sand

My mom, pop, & me.

Itsuko Taniguchi

A child's poem about the evacuation. MANZANAR FREE PRESS

Don't remember how many blankets we had. We had no nightclothes to change into, as the luggage was not unloaded that night from the train. Can't remember what we slept in; it was very cold and bleak."

The Army modeled Manzanar and the other nine war relocation facilities on the simple camps it was building to temporarily house millions of soldiers training to fight in World War II. Because of the military style, people called the buildings where they slept "barracks." They called dining rooms "mess halls," and bathrooms "latrines."

The main part of Manzanar was one mile long and one mile wide. Some fourteen miles of dirt roads, which were treated with oil to hold down the dust, crisscrossed the camp. There were thirty-six blocks, and each block consisted of two rows of seven barracks, a recreation hall, a mess hall, a men's latrine and shower, a women's latrine and shower, a laundry, and an ironing room. In all, there were more than five hundred tarpaper barracks, and they all looked alike. Numbers identified each block, barracks, and room. For example, if someone said he lived at 10–14–1, it meant the tenth block, the fourteenth barracks, room number 1.

Newcomers going to their barracks. CLEM ALBERS/NATIONAL ARCHIVES

A drawing that appeared in the Manzanar Free Press, *April 25, 1942.*

Because the wood-and-tarpaper barracks were highly flammable, the blocks were separated by wide, open spaces called firebreaks. If fire broke out in one block, the firebreaks would keep it from spreading to the barracks in other blocks. A firebreak was identified by the block numbers on either side of it. For example, firebreak 14–15 was the open space between blocks 14 and 15.

The WRA hired 150 Caucasians to manage the camp. These men and women lived in apartments and dormitories clustered on the south side of camp, near the entrance. They ate in their own mess hall and relaxed in their own recreation hall. The Army sent 120 military policemen from Fort Ord, near Monterey, California, to guard the imprisoned Japanese Americans. The soldiers lived in barracks a half mile south of camp and were not allowed to enter Manzanar unless there was trouble. For twenty-four hours

Mr. Scorpion: STAY AWAY FROM MY DOOR

They're not beetles or crabs. They're scorpions. And their sting is not fatal—at least the small ones a few inches long which are going around camp.

If you see one coming—usually around moist spots—step on it and kill it.

Its sting is about as serious and poisonous as the average bee sting.

To treat a sting, apply moist baking soda or ammonia and report immediately to the hospital or clinic.

Large scorpions, 8 to 12 inches long; are dangerous; but none has been seen here as yet.

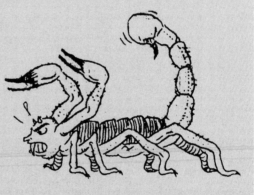

Manzanar residents had to beware of new kinds of pests, such as scorpions. MANZANAR FREE PRESS, MAY 9, 1942

a day sentries guarded the entrance, manned eight fifty-foot-high watchtowers, and patrolled the four miles of barbed-wire fence that surrounded the camp.

In the first months people tried to adjust to living in the small, crowded barracks. "One of the chief domestic problems of the early months resulted from inadequate housing," reported the *Manzanar Free Press*, a mimeographed newspaper published twice a week in the camp with the approval of WRA authoritites. "A one-room apartment measuring 20 by 25 feet was shared by two families of eight to ten people, who in many cases were total strangers to each other. Voices carried from one apartment to the next; folks tried in vain to sleep while listening to the heavy snoring of strange bedfellows."

In the noisy, cafeteria-style mess halls, people stood in long lines and ate at big tables. "It wasn't like having a meal made at home with loving hands," said a man, describing his first dinner at a camp mess hall. "The bread was very hard, apparently air toasted or something. The silverware and the dishes were not dried. They had aluminum ware—Army stuff. They were greasy to the touch. Just were dipped in warm water. The water we drank was dirty.

A typical line for lunch at a mess hall. People are standing in the building's shadow to avoid the hot sun.
Ansel Adams/Library of Congress

In the first weeks at Manzanar, few people liked the meals. They complained less after the mess halls began serving traditional Japanese foods, such as miso (a soup base), rice, soy sauce, and dakon (a long, white radish). CLEM ALBERS/NATIONAL ARCHIVES

. . . I couldn't get adjusted to the food. It was mostly canned, canned hash, canned meat. I had diarrhea. That stands out in my mind."

Although the people crowded into Manzanar shared a common heritage, they were different in many ways. They were rich as well as poor, educated and uneducated, English speaking and non–English speaking, city residents and farmers. The evacuees included Dr. James Goto and Dr. Masako Kusayanagi, a married couple from Los Angeles; Sister Mary Suzanne and

The mess halls were noisy and crowded with strangers. This atmosphere, parents complained, encouraged bad habits among their children. DOROTHEA LANGE/NATIONAL ARCHIVES

Girls doing their school lessons outdoors, on the shady side of a barracks.
DOROTHEA LANGE/
NATIONAL ARCHIVES

Sister Mary Bernadette, Catholic nuns of Japanese heritage; Toyo Miyatake, the photographer; Kuichiro Nishi, a stonemason and builder of rock gardens; F. M. Uyematsu, the owner of Star Nurseries in Montebello, California; and 103 orphans from San Francisco and Los Angeles, who lived in a special section of camp called Children's Village.

One boy did not have to be in Manzanar. He was Ralph Lazo, a sixteen-year-old Chicano from Los Angeles. Ralph wanted to join his Nisei friends, so he told his family he was going to Boy Scout camp and then told the Army he was part Japanese. The camp authorities recognized the boy was Mexican but allowed him to stay with friends. Lazo remained at Manzanar for two years, until he graduated from the camp high school and joined the Army.

The evacuation forced more than twenty thousand Nisei from numerous communities—from San Diego, California, all the way up the West Coast to Seattle, Washington—to leave their high schools and elementary schools weeks before the end of spring semester. Nearly 3,000 of these students were sent to Manzanar.

In the first months at the Owens Valley camp there were no schools. Instead, college-educated evacuees taught makeshift classes in bare rooms or on shady patches of ground outside. There were few texts, so teachers read to their classes from a single book or led discussions on topics such as the U.S. Constitution.

Manzanar's two hundred high school seniors worried about graduating on schedule. Thirteen students from Bainbridge Island, near Seattle, corresponded with their former teachers, finished their classwork, and received their diplomas in May. Other seniors worked during the summer to make up missed lessons and earn diplomas.

Under the leadership of Dr. Genevieve W. Carter, superintendent of

Boys in a classroom without furniture. DOROTHEA LANGE/NATIONAL ARCHIVES

There was only one high school, and some teenagers had a long walk home.
ANSEL ADAMS/ LIBRARY OF CONGRESS

education for the camp, Manzanar opened its nursery and elementary schools on September 15, 1942. A day earlier, the *Manzanar Free Press* had reported there were 450 nursery school and kindergarten children, 1,100 elementary school students, and 1,400 high school students, although only 895 had actually registered to attend. The high school opened September 28. It filled block seven: the mess hall, recreation building, and all fourteen barracks. Forty, fifty—as many as sixty—students crowded each classroom. The camp schools were part of the state education system, so they were required to teach foreign languages, sciences, mathematics, and other standard courses. But the teachers lacked lab equipment, blackboards, and even books. The classes in those first few months were not very good. By the second year, the schools had more equipment and classes were better.

Elementary school and kindergarten classes were held in barracks throughout the camp so that the younger children would be close to their homes. In the first weeks students sat on the floor or carried homemade benches to class. There were several days that winter when the uninsulated barracks were so cold that classes were canceled.

The newspaper article of September 14 also stated that only twenty-six of the fifty-nine Caucasian teachers who had been expected had reported to the camp. There was a shortage of teachers because few people wanted to work at a prison camp in the desert. Moreover, the salaries were low. Professional teachers were paid $1,620 a year, much less than they could earn in the labor-starved factories in the cities.

The schools made up for the shortage by hiring evacuees as teachers' assistants. The assistants did the same work as white teachers, but they were paid only sixteen dollars a month. Few Nisei had ever gone to college to become teachers, because prejudice kept most American schools from hiring Asian educators.

No one that first year was happy with the schools, especially the students. Sue Kunitomi remembers asking Tetsuo, her twelve-year-old brother,

School's out. There were numerous kindergarten and elementary schools for young children.
DOROTHEA LANGE/NATIONAL ARCHIVES

how he liked his classes. "There are no chairs, no desks, no supplies," he replied. Then the boy asked a difficult question. "What's the use of studying American history when we're behind barbed wire?"

The schools seemed to be full of strangers. Manzanar's students had attended 212 different high schools and 148 different elementary schools. The editors of *Our World*, the 1943 Manzanar High School yearbook, listed the names of the schools—Sacred Heart, Thomas Jefferson, Theodore Roosevelt—from which each senior would have graduated if not for the evacuation. Boys and girls who had known each other before the war often banded together. They called themselves the Venice Boys, San Pedro Club, Roosevelt High Gang, or Hollywood Bunch—names that identified where they once had lived or had gone to school.

Dispirited students at Manzanar were not interested in their classes. One man described the changes he saw in his sixteen-year-old younger brother. "He attended North Hollywood High and Emerson Junior High, West Hollywood, L.A. He likes math. He used to get straight As in it in North Hollywood." But since coming to camp, the boy's brother continued, "Even if he is threatened with an F, he won't hand in a notebook. . . . He doesn't care about marks."

Conditions at Manzanar caused some boys and girls to become sullen and others to become aggressive. Boys kicked in doors and ripped tarpaper off buildings. Some yelled at their teachers. "I hate you. I hate all Caucasians!" a fourth grader screamed in class before bursting into tears.

Excerpt from an editorial that appeared in the MANZANAR FREE PRESS, *July 4, 1942.*

EDITORIAL
Independence Day—1942

Fourth of July this year will have poignant meaning and value for an America gripped in a death struggle for the very principles affirmed in the Declaration of Independence.

For American citizens of Japanese ancestry herded into camps and guarded by the bayoneted sentries of their own country, it will be a doubly strange and bewildering day. . . . But let us think twice, lost in our understandable and human bitterness, [before] we dismiss this day with an ironic shrug and a customary wisecrack. . . .

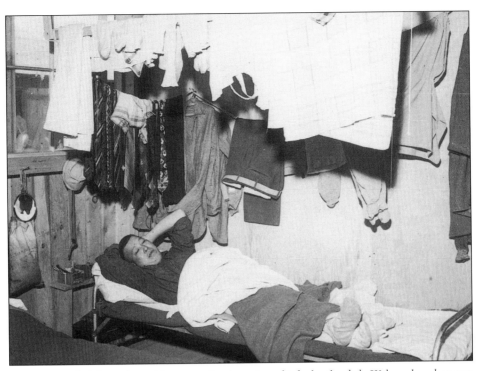

At first no one had closets, chests of drawers, or furniture of any kind other than beds. With nowhere else to put his clothing, this man hung it on a rope strung across the room. CLEM ALBERS/NATIONAL ARCHIVES

The adults were also unhappy as they tried to adjust to the new regulations and routines of life behind barbed wire. The fishermen, merchants, and farmers confined at Manzanar were accustomed to laboring long hours for five, six, and even seven days a week. What could these hard-working people do, locked in this dusty camp?

Some evacuees got busy furnishing their bare rooms. Men and boys searched the camp for scrap lumber or stole wood from the barracks still under construction to make shelves, tables, and chairs.

The WRA authorities wanted Manzanar's residents to do all the work necessary to sustain the camp, and so the Nisei and Issei unloaded trucks at the warehouses, or cooked, served meals, and washed dishes in the mess halls. More than five hundred people worked in the camp maintenance department picking up garbage, repairing boilers, and fixing water pipes. Dr. Goto, a former surgeon at Los Angeles General Hospital, was chief of staff at Manzanar's 250-bed hospital. His wife, Dr. Kusayanagi, also worked on the hospital staff. On April 16, 1942, she delivered Kenji Ogawa, the first baby born in the camp.

The farmers repaired old irrigation ditches and pruned the long-neglected apple and pear trees in the orchards that gave Manzanar its name. They then plowed three hundred acres of nearby land and planted corn, cucumbers, melons, radishes, turnips, tomatoes, and squash, which would be served in the mess halls.

Merchants confined in Manzanar were busy as well. By asking each resident for a five-dollar investment, they collected enough money to open a large store selling clothing, shoes, cosmetics, sewing supplies, crackers, soft

Farmer plowing a field. The residents grew much of their own food.
Ansel Adams/Library of Congress

drinks, and toys. The co-op quickly proved successful and added additional services, such as a laundry, movie theater, and shoe repair, barber, and beauty shops.

The WRA also organized a police force of 115 Issei and Nisei men, who were supervised by two Caucasian law officers. Armed with nightsticks and identified by white armbands marked by the word POLICE, members of the force patrolled the camp. They were aided by the Peace Committee, a group of young judo experts led by martial arts instructor Seigoro Murakami, who removed troublemakers from parties and broke up fights at ball games.

The camp administrators paid workers small salaries depending on their job skills. The top salary was nineteen dollars a month, but few people earned more than sixteen dollars a month. Many evacuees were angry that they were not paid fairly for their work. The resentment over low pay, combined with anger over the evacuation, led to a deadly riot.

December 6, 1942, was a Sunday, a day that was usually quiet. But late that afternoon, Director Merritt made an urgent call to Captain Martyn L. Hall, the commanding officer of the 322nd Military Police Escort and Guard Company, which guarded the camp. Merritt explained that a mob had gathered in the firebreak near the administration building, and there might be trouble. Captain Hall and twelve soldiers, armed with shotguns and machine guns, rushed the half mile to the camp entrance.

An estimated two thousand people had gathered on that cold afternoon to protest the arrest of Harry Ueno. He was the leader of a local union of kitchen workers and an outspoken critic of the WRA authorities. Ueno had been accused of beating Fred Tayama, a leader of evacuees who were loyal to the administrators and a suspected FBI informer.

The angry crowd denounced Tayama as an *inu*, a Japanese word that can mean either "dog" or "traitor." The protesters had armed themselves with hatchets, knives, hammers, stones, and clubs. Shouting "Free Harry" and

Back to barbarism

The thrill of pride that surges down our spine when we view the miracles wrought in a few months' time is dampened when we hear of increasing cases of vandalism and mob rule here.

Ruffians who have taken the law into their own clenched fists have escaped with a reprimand from the police who were powerless to do more than maintain surveillance. This was due to the lack of any recognized court of law that could enforce order.

Now the situation has changed. Even though it is temporary, we have a judicial committee empowered to pass judgment. Every case of gang warfare and unrefereed fisticuffs should be severely punished. The Manzanar Free Press promises full publicity in these cases.

If the prospects of cooling their heels in the iron cage will not deter these hotheads, perhaps the threat of having their names smeared on the pages of a documentary newspaper will make them hold back that punch.

We cannot revert to barbarism!

This editorial in the Manzanar Free Press, *August 3, 1942, hints at the divisions among the evacuees that led to a riot four months later.*

"Kill the *inu*," several hundred people rushed to the jail, while a smaller group ran to the hospital to "take care of" Tayama.

The men searched the hospital room by room looking for Tayama but could not find him. The nurses had hidden their patient in a storage closet beneath a stack of blankets.

At the jail hundreds of men and boys confronted Captain Hall and his armed troops. The cursing mob pressed in on the soldiers. The GIs quickly pulled gas masks over their faces and fired tear gas into the crowd. Choking and crying from the bitter gas, the rioters retreated a hundred feet.

Several young men began pushing a parked car toward the soldiers. As the automobile gathered speed, the troops raised their guns. The driverless vehicle veered aside when the men stopped pushing and turned to run. The soldiers fired into the crowd. Eleven men and boys fell.

"A classmate, Jimmy Ito, was shot and killed," remembered teenager Grace Nakamura. "It was a terrifying experience." The next day another man died from his wounds. He was twenty-one-year-old James Kanagawa from Tacoma, Washington.

Soldiers patrolled Manzanar's streets until dawn. Evacuees occupied mess halls, ringing the dinner gongs that were usually rung only to signal mealtime. This dark and cold night they sounded like church bells tolling for the dead.

The following day was Monday, and the camp schools opened as usual. But some of the high school boys, angry at the killing of Jimmy Ito, locked teachers in classrooms and wrote threats and obscene words on blackboards. The teachers dismissed classes and all the camp schools were closed for the next five weeks.

The *Manzanar Free Press* ceased publication for several weeks after the riot, and camp administrators did not allow the newspaper to write about the riot until a year later. The newspaper published a short article on the anniversary of the riot. It said little about the details of that night. But it did say that the "strife and difficulties" at Manzanar and other relocation camps "reflects on the basic difficulty of any group to maintain a normal life under crowded circumstances."

WRA officials thought there would be more riots at Manzanar unless they separated the pro-Japanese evacuees from the pro-American evacuees, and reduced the number of people in the camp. In early 1943, they sent the leaders of the two factions to special high-security prison camps in Arizona. The officials also created a loyalty test, which they called "Application for Leave Clearance." Evacuees who answered the questions correctly could leave the camps. They would not be allowed to return to their West Coast homes, but they could move to other cities to live and work. The people who gave the wrong answers would be considered disloyal and sent to Tule Lake Relocation Center in northern California. The WRA authorities required every evacuee over age seventeen to take the test.

People leaving for Tule Lake. TOYO MIYATAKE/MIYATAKE STUDIO

Two questions, 27 and 28, caused a lot of problems. Question 27 asked if the person was willing to go to war to defend the United States. This angered Nisei men, who were incredulous at being asked to fight—and perhaps die—for a country that had taken away their freedom.

And question 28 was even more insulting to the evacuees. It asked them to swear allegiance to the United States and renounce allegiance to Japan and its emperor. The emperor at that time was a supremely important figure among the Japanese. Asking his subjects to forsake him was as serious as asking priests to forsake God. And because the Issei were not allowed to become American citizens, renouncing Japan would leave them without citizenship in any country.

At first many evacuees refused to answer the two questions, because they did not trust WRA officials. People believed that if they answered no, they would be separated from family and friends and sent to another camp. Or they would be sent to Japan. The evacuees argued among themselves over what to do. The arguments destroyed friendships and split families. Eventually, most people decided to answer the questions, saying yes to both. Those who answered no were dubbed "No-Nos." In the summer of 1943 the WRA sent 2,200 Manzanar No-Nos to the Tule Lake Relocation Center in northern California, where they joined several thousand No-Nos removed from the other camps. Eventually, nearly 4,500 people from the Tule Lake center would be sent to Japan.

The children moving to the northern California camp with their parents did not understand why they had to leave once again. "Two came to me," recalled an elementary school teacher, "and said, 'We don't want to go to Tule Lake and to Japan. We want to stay here in America. We don't want to go to a Japanese school. Reading and writing Japanese is too hard for us. We want to go to this kind of school.'"

By the end of 1943 half of Manzanar's original population had left

**SPECIAL . . . .
ANNIVERSARY EDITION**

MANZANAR Free Press

Volume III, No. 23   **Saturday, March 20, 1943**   **Manzanar, California**

This anniversary edition commemorates the arrival, one year earlier, of the first evacuees who came to help build the camp.

Owens Valley. Many went to Tule Lake. Some young men had even joined the Army. Dozens of other young men and women went east to attend college. And both young and middle-aged people moved to Midwestern and Eastern cities to live and work.

"Right after the riot, Christmas was so dismal," Sue Kunitomi recalled. "I promised myself I would leave before I spent another Christmas there in Manzanar. I left in October of 1943." Sue moved to Madison, Wisconsin, where she worked as a clerk, taking orders for a mail-order cheese company. Her mother and younger brother stayed in the camp until the end of the war.

View of the camp from one of the Army watchtowers. ANSEL ADAMS/LIBRARY OF CONGRESS

4

The Final Months at Manzanar

The five thousand evacuees who remained at Manzanar after 1943 were people like Sue Kunitomi's mother and younger brother—that is, older Issei and school-age Nisei who did not want to go to unfamiliar cities in the East. They wanted to return to their West Coast homes. So waiting for the war to end, people confined at Manzanar settled into a routine of work, school, and play. Many evacuees enthusiastically celebrated national holidays and participated in sports. These activities were fun as well as ways of stressing their loyalty to America.

During the last week of April 1944, Manzanar gave a big parade for Boys and Girls Week. This was a holiday similar to Mother's Day and Father's Day that was popular in the United States in the 1920s, 1930s, and 1940s.

On the first day of the holiday, at 2 P.M., a thousand schoolchildren lined up four abreast in firebreak 14–15. Hundreds more gathered in groups, carrying banners, wearing armbands, or dressed in uniforms that identified them as members of various clubs such as the Junior Red Cross, High Y, or Boy Scouts. Majorettes twirled shiny batons, and the band marched and played their instruments while the spectators enthusiastically sang "The

Star-Spangled Banner," "America the Beautiful," and the official Manzanar song, "We Are Building for Tomorrow."

The Nisei and Sansei participated in the same pastimes as other young Americans. They had long enjoyed sports like baseball, softball, football, and basketball, but these seemed even more important during the war years.

Dan Tsurutani, an evacuee at Manzanar, described seeing fathers and daughters playing ball together. "A group of young girls on the sidelines—none over sixteen—were shouting encouragement to the batter. A ten-year-old girl was keeping score.

"'Hey, Shizu, knock that apple over your dad's head!'

"'Sato-san can't pitch. He's squeaking like a rusty gate.'

Majorettes pose for this high school yearbook photograph with the Sierra Nevada as a backdrop.
TOYO MIYATAKE/MIYATAKE STUDIO

Girls, who played on a team called the Chick-a-dees, practice for a softball game.
Dorothea Lange/National Archives

"*'Yoshi, yoshi, shikkari shite nagero.'* (Put some fire behind the ball.)

"*'Sa! Kitzao, toreyo!'* (It's coming! Get it!)

"*'Doikoisho ah, dameda!'* (Gosh, I missed it!)

"Hobbling fathers playing with their peppy daughters with mothers watching from the shade of the barracks and rocking with laughter—this, indeed, is a drastic change in the older folks' behavior toward their children. This is not an isolated case, because games of this nature are being played every evening by several teams in various parts of the center."

Such sights, Tsurutani explained, were once unusual because "Japanese fathers seldom played with their daughters in public." And parents had

Basketball had to be played outdoors until the evacuees built an auditorium in 1943.
FRANCIS STEWART/NATIONAL ARCHIVES

Adult baseball games attracted hundreds of spectators. Former Fish Harbor residents were among the best players. ANSEL ADAMS/LIBRARY OF CONGRESS

discouraged their daughters' interest in sports by calling them *otemba,* or tomboys.

Everyone in camp seemed to be playing baseball. A fifth grader wrote a description of a game for his school newspaper, the *Manzanar Whirlwind.*

"We elementary pupils have started and finished our baseball game. We played hard, and those who did not play rooted and cheered. But above all we tried to be good sportsmen. The sixth grades from 9–15 were the champions. Fine work, nine–fifteens. We are proud of you. John Osajma, 5–15th 5th."

In addition to sports, young Japanese Americans enjoyed movies and music. They looked forward to the weekends, when they could watch movies such as *The Road to Singapore, Star Spangled Rhythm, The Pride of the Yankees, How Green Was My Valley, Hold That Ghost,* and *Jungle Book.* Another favorite weekend activity was dancing to the songs of Frank Sinatra and the dance bands of Duke Ellington, Benny Goodman, and Tommy and Jimmy Dorsey. Evacuees organized their own bands, too. One of the most popular was called the Jive Bombers.

Young people went to movies and dances dressed like other American teenagers. Girls wore blouses and skirts and boys jeans and T-shirts. Some of the more daring boys wore zoot suits, a radical fashion of the time. Zoot suits had become popular in the late 1930s among young Chicano and black men in Los Angeles and New York. The trousers were baggy at the hips and

Dancing was popular among young evacuees. Library of Congress

Manzanar residents making camouflage nets for the Army. NATIONAL ARCHIVES.

tapered snugly at the ankles. The jacket had wide padded shoulders and wide lapels and hung down to the knees.

There was no television in those days, but camp residents listened to the radio in the evenings and read the 2,200 copies of Los Angeles newspapers, such as the *Times* and *Examiner,* that came to the camp each week. Evacuees closely followed the progress of the war against Japan and Germany. They were especially interested in news about the Army's 442nd Combat Battalion, a Nisei outfit fighting in Italy. Forty-two Manzanar men had volunteered for the new battalion when it was created in 1943. And more joined the Army when the Selective Service System, which had stopped drafting

Warehouse workers keeping track of the many items needed by the evacuees.
ANSEL ADAMS/ LIBRARY OF CONGRESS

Japanese Americans after the bombing of Pearl Harbor, resumed drafting them in early 1944. Residents erected a big board in the center of camp on which were listed the names of sons—and daughters—serving in the armed forces.

The men of the 442nd fought skillfully and bravely. They won more medals and honors than any other Army unit, but they also suffered more casualties than other units. Families whose sons were killed hung embroidered gold stars on their walls or in their windows. People in the relocation camps felt that the Nisei soldiers were fighting for the honor of all Japanese Americans.

Life at Manzanar settled into a predictable routine. Nights beneath the vast star-filled sky were peaceful. The evacuees had made their rooms in the tarpaper barracks more comfortable by covering their walls with plasterboard and their floors with linoleum to keep out the cold and the dust.

Students finished homework, while others read, sewed, or wrote letters until it was time for bed.

A typical day began at 4:30 A.M., when cooks and mess-hall workers awoke to get ready for work. At 6:45 A.M., the *clang, clang, clang* of mess-hall gongs announced breakfast. Lights popped on in the barracks, and doors began to slam as people hurried back and forth to latrines and showers. The smell of frying bacon filled the mess halls. Breakfast often included pancakes, grapefruit, corn flakes, coffee, tea, and milk. Afterward the children joined friends to walk to school, and adults went to work.

By the third summer, 1944, the Manzanar farmers were planting crops on six thousand acres and raising cattle, pigs, chickens, and ducks. Other WRA camps had farms, too, but the Manzanar farm was the largest. It sold

Girls hanging makeshift curtains.
CLEM ALBERS/
NATIONAL ARCHIVES

Merritt Park, the largest park created by evacuees. ANSEL ADAMS/LIBRARY OF CONGRESS

vegetables and animals to the other nine relocation camps as well as to Los Angeles markets, earning over a million dollars that year. The money belonged to the federal government, which used it to pay the camp's expenses.

When not busy at their regular jobs, Manzanar residents built rock gardens and planted flowers beside their barracks. They created a large community park, called Merritt Park, by planting trees and roses, digging fish ponds, and building a gazebo, a rustic wooden bridge, and a Japanese-style teahouse. The WRA staff allowed F. M. Uyematsu to visit his nursery in Montebello and bring back a thousand Japanese cherry trees, which he planted in front of Children's Village, where the orphans who had been evacuated from San Francisco and Los Angeles lived. By 1944 Manzanar looked very different from the way it had that bleak spring two years earlier. "In most ways it was a totally equipped American small town," recalled Jeanne Wakatsuki Houston, a journalist who was seven years old when her family was confined in Manzanar. It was "complete with schools, churches, Boy Scouts, beauty parlors, neighborhood gossip, fire and police departments, glee clubs, softball leagues, Abbott and Costello movies, tennis courts, and traveling shows."

While life at Manzanar had improved considerably, the residents there jumped at their first opportunity to return home. Soon after Franklin D. Roosevelt won his fourth presidential election, in November 1944, he removed the ban barring Japanese Americans from the West Coast.

The baseball diamonds at Manzanar were silent by the summer of 1945.

Saying goodbye to people leaving Manzanar for jobs in the Midwest.
Ansel Adams/Library of Congress

Workers dismantle one of the barracks. Several barracks were moved to the neighboring towns of Lone Pine and Independence, where they still stand today. TOYO MIYATAKE/MIYATAKE STUDIOS

Long lines of people no longer stood outside the mess halls at mealtimes. Only a few elderly people, who had no money, no family, and nowhere else to go, remained in the tarpaper barracks. Eventually, churches and other charitable groups found them homes. Manzanar officially closed on November 21, 1945. Michiko Mizumoto, a young evacuee at Manzanar, published a poem in 1943 that anticipated the day of freedom. Her poem ended with these lines:

> . . . the dawn is approaching,
> When these, who have learned and suffered in silent courage;
> Better, wiser, for the unforgettable interlude of detention,
> Shall trod on free sod again,
> Side by side peacefully with those who sneered at the
> Dust storms.
> Sweat days.
> Yellow people,
> Exiles.

People at the Manzanar Pilgrimage on April 28, 2001. Michael L. Cooper

5

Manzanar Today

As I stood near the sentry houses on the Saturday of the 2001 Manzanar Pilgrimage, several buses pulled slowly onto the dirt road. I looked up at the bus windows and saw Japanese American faces peering out at the landscape. Their somber expressions reminded me of old photographs I had seen of evacuees first coming to this place in 1942. The tall buses drove past the sentry houses on their way to the cemetery at the western edge of the camp.

On foot, I followed the same road past the auditorium and toward the snow-capped mountains. Along the way, mindful of the National Park Service's strict rules against disturbing anything, I passed artifacts from the war years—old rock gardens, stone foundations, concrete walkways, and rusted water pipes sticking out of the sand.

The walk took about thirty minutes and ended at a gravel parking area that was full of buses and cars. Hundreds of people had gathered at the old camp cemetery, where a simple wooden fence encloses several graves and a gleaming white obelisk. Japanese picture words, called *ireito*, on two sides of the concrete shaft state that the tower was "erected by the Manzanar Japanese" in August 1943 as a memorial to the dead—a "Soul Consoling Tower."

Flags near the monument identified the names of each of the ten reloca-

A young woman walks past flags fluttering in the Owens Valley wind. Each flag represents a relocation camp. MICHAEL L. COOPER

Sue Kunitomi Embrey, on the right, was confined in Manzanar as a teenager. Gann Matsuda, on the left, is from Los Angeles. MICHAEL L. COOPER

tion camps—Amache, Gila River, Heart Mountain, Jerome, Manzanar, Minidoka, Poston, Rohwer, Topaz, and Tule Lake. There's an eleventh flag for a camp that was under the jurisdiction of the Justice Department at Crystal City, Texas, where four thousand people were imprisoned. This was one of the camps to which the FBI agents sent the people, such as the Fish Harbor fishermen, whom they arrested after Pearl Harbor was bombed. The camp also held 660 Peruvians of Japanese heritage who had been exiled by their country, and 600 Hawaiians of Japanese ancestry.

At the cemetery hundreds of people milled about. Many of them were

Nisei and Sansei, but there were also African Americans, Mexican Americans, Native Americans, and Caucasians. People on a flatbed truck, elevated above the crowd, took turns speaking into the public address system about what this spot, this day, meant to them. One man introduced the men and women who had made the five-day run from Los Angeles.

That day I met Sue Kunitomi Embrey. We talked about her life after the war. She explained that she had returned to Los Angeles in 1948 and taken a job with the Los Angeles Health Department. She had married a Caucasian from Waco, Texas, and they raised three children. A few years later Sue began working to make the memory of Manzanar survive for generations: In 1969 she helped organize the first Manzanar Pilgrimage. And the former evacuee has worked tirelessly for decades to make the old relocation camp a National Historic Site. On this day, attending her thirty-second pilgrimage, Sue sat under

A group of young musicians play taiko drums. These drums, which can be as big as a barrel or as small as a hatbox, are traditionally used in Japanese Buddhist ceremonies. MICHAEL L. COOPER

Ondo dancers at the end of the Manzanar ceremony. Elderly people attending the pilgrimage remembered doing the ondo dance when they were children confined in the relocation camp. MICHAEL L. COOPER

an umbrella shaded from the hot sun as she watched the two-hour ceremony.

It began with a *taiko* group playing barrel-shaped drums. Then a rabbi, several Protestant ministers, and Catholic, Shinto, and Buddhist priests took turns offering prayers by the obelisk. The ceremony ended with an *ondo* dance. This is a traditional Japanese folk dance in which people line up behind a lead dancer. They slowly snaked around the cemetery, swaying and gesturing with their hands. Both the *ondo* dance and the *taiko* drums are traditional features of Buddhist ceremonies to remember the dead.

The memorial service invoked the memory of people buried in the cemetery as well as the memory of one of the most serious mistakes in our nation's

Shinto priests preparing to conduct memorial services at the obelisk. Shinto is an Japanese religion that is more than two thousand years old. MICHAEL L. COOPER

history. Today, most people understand that it was wrong to uproot 112,000 Japanese Americans from their homes and confine them in relocation camps. These people never threatened America. Rather, like millions of other immigrants who came to this country, they were hard-working and glad to be raising their families in the land many Asians called the Golden Mountain.

But the mass evacuation tarnished that golden image. After Japan bombed Pearl Harbor, prejudice and fear allowed America to betray basic principles of equal and fair treatment for all of its people. Japanese Americans, simply because of their heritage, were treated as traitors, not to be trusted but to be banished. Such unfair treatment is long remembered by people who have experienced it; and it should be long remembered by every American.

Many people recalled the forced evacuation of World War II after the September 11, 2001, terrorist attacks on the World Trade Center in New York City and the Pentagon in Washington, D.C., which killed more than three thousand people. This was the worst attack on United States soil since the Japanese bombed Pearl Harbor in 1941. Nineteen men from the Mideast carried out the September 11 attacks. Some angry Americans singled out people of Mideastern heritage—and even people who only looked as if they were of Mideastern heritage—for verbal and physical abuse. Their businesses were boycotted. Some were denied passage on airliners. One man in Arizona was murdered in what investigators believe was a hate crime.

Despite widespread fear of terrorism, few Americans suggested imprisoning people of Mideastern heritage in relocation camps. Too many remembered the grave injustices against Japanese Americans nearly sixty years earlier. The mistakes of the past have helped Americans understand that the United States is a diverse country, populated by immigrants from all parts of the world. Everyone, regardless of skin color, ethnicity, or heritage, can be a good and loyal American.

End Notes

Most of my research for this book was from primary sources. All the records of the War Relocation Authority, an agency which existed only during the war years, are kept in the National Archives in Washington, D.C. Among the files I found most useful were the microfilm records of the *Manzanar Free Press.* I looked at every issue of that newspaper for a better understanding of day-to-day events in the camp. Although evacuees published the newspaper, camp authorities did not allow them to cover all the news. For example, there was no coverage of the Manzanar riot. Other useful files were the community analyst's reports. The analyst, Morris Opler, interviewed the evacuees, asking how they felt about the evacuation and about the relocation camp. Opler promised not to reveal the names of the people he interviewed so they would talk frankly.

My trip across the country to the Owens Valley in April 2001 was an invaluable part of my research. I met two people who told me things I had not found in books. I had corresponded with one of them, Sue Kunitomi Embrey, before my trip. She is the chairwoman of the Manzanar Pilgrimage Committee. I met the other, Wilbur Sato, at the little motel where I stayed in Independence, California. His room was next to mine, and we spent an afternoon sitting out front and talking about his two years at Manzanar. Both Wilbur and Sue were at Manzanar as teenagers.

There are several books specifically about Manzanar. One is Jeanne Wakatsuki Houston and James D. Houston's *Farewell to Manzanar: A True Story of Japanese American Experience During and After the World War II Internment* (New York: Bantam, 1995; Houghton Mifflin, 2002). It is a beautifully written account of the years Jeanne spent as a child in the camp. Another, simply titled *Manzanar* (New York: Times Books, 1988), with an introduction by John Hersey and a text by John Armor and Peter Wright, features the Ansel Adams photographs previously published in his unpopular book *Born Free and Equal: Photographs of the Loyal Japanese-Americans at Manzanar Relocation Center, Inyo County, California* (New York: U.S. Camera, 1944). Adams's photographs are matched with Toyo Miyatake's in *Two Views of Manzanar* (Los Angeles: Frederick S. Wight Art Gallery, 1978).

There are many books about the evacuation and the relocation camps. Some of the best include Audrie Girdner and Anne Loftins's *The Great Betrayal: The Evacuation of the Japanese-Americans During World War II* (New York: Macmillan, 1969); Page Smith's *Democracy on Trial: The Japanese American Evacuation and Relocation in World War II* (New York: Simon & Schuster, 1995); and Michi Weglyn's *Years of Infamy: The Untold Story of America's Concentration Camps* (New York: Morrow, 1976).

Internet Resources

http://www.janm.org/ The Japanese American National Museum in Los Angeles. This site has numerous links to related web sites.

http://www.lcweb.loc.gov/rr/print/ The Prints and Photographs Division of the Library of Congress has online exhibits of both Ansel Adams's and Dorothea Lange's photographs of Manzanar.

Index

Page numbers in **bold** type refer to photographs.